So spry in the nineties! May that
be your goal as it is [...]
alice Eastwood –

For Roger and Joan –
from
mother.

John Thomas Howell

Susanne Bryant Dakin

Alice Eastwood

The Perennial Adventure

A TRIBUTE TO

Alice Eastwood

1859 - 1953

BY

Susanna Bryant Dakin

SAN FRANCISCO

CALIFORNIA ACADEMY OF SCIENCES

MCMLIV

QK
31
E27
D3

Friends:

How GRATEFUL we should be to those responsible for this beautiful little volume that is so adequate a tribute to Alice Eastwood! Members of the Marin Garden Club first thought of this way of honoring the memory of their dear friend. In executing their plan, they have had the advice and cooperation of the officers of the California Academy of Sciences. The entire proceeds are assigned to the Alice Eastwood Hall of Botany Fund. To Mr. Lawton Kennedy goes the credit for his dedicated service in making this volume so quickly available and for embodying the text in so choice a manner, and to John Falter for enhancing it with two delightful drawings.

I should like to emphasize the adequateness of this little book: first, by telling you something Miss Eastwood would never have said; and second, by telling you something Miss Eastwood did say.

No member of a botany class or a garden club ever heard Miss Eastwood refuse to examine a plant with the disparaging remark, "Oh, I've seen that flower before." Whenever or wherever she might have been shown a flower, no matter how common and how weedy, the truth and the beauty exhibited by the structural formation of that flower would have at once inspired a spirited lesson on what she saw and what it meant, just as if she had never before seen so common a weed. It was this appreciation of truth and beauty in all botanical manifestations that was the foremost principle of her life. In her high school valedictory that is reprinted in this volume, she set truth and the search of truth as the loadstar of her life, and as teacher and scientist she remained faithful to that course in all the years that followed.

In her pursuit of truth, Alice Eastwood strove to cultivate the essential, to weed out the unessential, so that the garden of her life would be open and uncluttered. How well I recall her attempt to teach me this principle. A minor editorial detail was being discussed and the merits of two styles were being compared. At last, to close my argument, I remarked: "What you propose will not be consistent." "Consistency," she flung back, "is the bane of small minds." Indeed, consistency with unessentials was never a part of Alice Eastwood's life.

What she gained was an enviable freedom for thought and action. Her fearless botanical journeying into deserts and mountains was one of the results, and these trips relate her in fact and in spirit to the early explorers of our country, for whom she had a fervent admiration. How exceptionally appropriate is it that her botanical paper chosen for reproduction in this volume should be the one on "Early Botanical Explorers . . ."!

If we throw to the wind the trivial conventions that shackle us to earth, our lives too can become as vital, as real, as full as hers. Little wonder that Dr. Robert C. Miller could write of Miss Eastwood as he did in his introductory remarks to Carol Green Wilson's biography: "A blithe spirit that is ageless, living in a world of discovery that is ever new. . . . Men have sought in vain the fountain of perpetual youth; what they needed instead was the fountain of perennial adventure."

JOHN THOMAS HOWELL
California Academy of Sciences
DECEMBER 2, 1953

Author's Preface

CAROL GREEN WILSON has been generous in allowing me to glean information from her forthcoming biography, titled "Alice Eastwood's Wonderland" and completed only a little while before the eminent botanist's death at ninety-four on October 30, 1953. In this book Alice Eastwood's honors, her world-wide associations, her scientific and literary achievements, her exciting botanical expeditions and her observant travels are detailed. The total is imposing indeed. It can only be intimated in this sketch based on Mrs. Wilson's book—a sketch written and published as one of many memorials to a unique human being; no less a dedicated scientist than a well-loved woman.

Always a helpful person is John Thomas Howell, who succeeded Miss Eastwood as Curator of Botany at the California Academy of Sciences when she retired at the age of ninety, after fifty-seven years of service there. He has chosen illustrations out of photographs in his possession; and edited the manuscript for Academy publication.

Besides the outline of Alice Eastwood's life,* we include her own understanding account of "Early Botanical Explorers on the Pacific Coast."** Her spirit is kindred to Archibald Menzies, botanist and surgeon of Vancouver's round-the-world expedition (1790–1795), who first noted and collected the Coast Redwood growing near Santa Cruz; to the young Scot, David Douglas of intrepid spirit and untimely end; to Thomas Coulter, who first penetrated the rocky fastnesses of the Santa Lucia Mountains to discover the Santa Lucia Fir and Big-cone Pine; to Thomas Nuttall, who named and described our picturesque sycamore, the *aliso* of the Spanish Californians. Each of these explorers sought and found "the fountain of perennial adventure." We envy and we honor them.

*Originally written for the Bulletin of the Garden Club of America; published in shortened form, January, 1954.

**Published in the December 1939 issue of the California Historical Society Quarterly. This was one of more than three hundred botanical writings by Alice Eastwood published during her lifetime and listed in *Proceedings of the California Academy of Sciences (Fourth Series) Vol. XXV Alice Eastwood Semi-Centennial Publications, San Francisco, published by the Academy 1943-1949.*

The Perennial Adventure

A Tribute to Alice Eastwood

THERE IS A SIMPLICITY and an inevitability in Alice Eastwood's life history. Everything, even disappointment, became grist for her ever-grinding inner mill. Everybody who entered her life, even briefly, seemed to contribute eventually to the creation of this integrated personality. A botanical analogy can be drawn from the three distinct eras of a long lifetime. In the Canadian childhood was planted the seed of a true vocation; in Colorado this seed rooted and sprouted in the dark ground of poverty and hardship; in California it flowered for all the world to see.

Her biographer tells us that Alice Eastwood was the only woman starred for distinction in every volume of "American Men of Science," published during her lifetime. Her most prized citation came the year of her retirement, in the form of an invitation to serve as Honorary President of the Seventh International Botanical Congress, meeting in Sweden in 1950. There she went, flying alone at the age of ninety-one! Though fêted in queenly fashion, her happiest moment was not one of personal tribute. It happened during a day of pilgrimage to the home of Carolus Linnaeus, the great eighteenth century scholar. Here she, small and frail, was invited to sit in the ancient chair which *he* used while writing the source book of modern systematic botany.

Miss Eastwood's traveling hat is noteworthy. She who once

I

earned a living with the needle, never had time to think of
clothes. So some friends helped her in assembling a wardrobe for
the trip to Sweden. One, a fashionable milliner, planted grey silk
mushrooms (complete with *lamellae*) on a grey sailor hat. This
seemed aprópos, since even the Health Officer customarily con-
sulted Miss Eastwood about the edibility of wild mushrooms.
With the new hat tilted on her snowy hair, a harmonizing coat
and dress; with Irish eyes still twinkling, it is no wonder that she
once again was voted "Sweetheart of the Year" by the San Francisco Business Men's Garden Club—a perennial honor which she
received in a city faithful to its favorites.

For a serious scientist to have frivolous moments and quantities
of friends—this is a phenomenon. Contrast the Curie *salon* as the
extreme of austerity, containing a straight chair each for Pierre
and Marie, to Alice Eastwood's home wherever she made it. Her
living-room always became a gathering place for congenial spirits, even when it was her only room—in days of poverty or illness.
Always there was good talk and, often, good food prepared by
the hostess. A colleague once intimated that her contribution to
science might be lessened by an unfailing interest in fellow human
beings, by the love and time she lavished on her friends and their
concerns. She answered, expressing a lifelong philosophy, "My
desire is to help, not to shine."

Alice Eastwood was born on January 19, 1859, in Toronto,
Canada, of an Irish mother and an English father. Her relatives
on both sides lacked worldly goods, in most instances, but were
endowed through the generations with integrity and education.

A grandfather had been a rebel in youth, and later became a founder of the Unitarian Church in Toronto with her mother's cousin, Dr. Joseph Workman, Canada's leading alienist and neurologist.

Her early years passed securely and happily in a rather macabre setting—the grounds of the Toronto Asylum for the Insane. Here Dr. Workman served as superintendent, and Colin Eastwood as steward. When little Alice was six her lovely mother died, leaving the little family rudderless and adrift. For a time the three children (Alice, the oldest; Catherine, four; and Sidney, only fourteen months old) stayed with their uncle, Dr. William Eastwood, at his country place on Highland Creek.

Here was planted the seed of Alice Eastwood's lifelong interest in botany. She roved freely and independently in the meadows and nearby woods, sometimes with cousins but more often alone. Her uncle recognized a kindred spirit, even in one so young, and taught her names she never forgot—like the wild raspberry which she learned to call *Rubus odoratus,* and *Mitchella repens* the red partridge berry.

In 1867 she returned to live with her father (now a storekeeper) and took considerable responsibility for the younger children, even at eight years of age. She made friends and distinguished herself at the neighborhood school. Elizabeth Fry's "The Prisoner's Friend" was awarded to Alice Eastwood for excellence in spelling. But the father's store did not prosper and, once again, the family circle was broken. Mr. Eastwood took little Sidney out west, and placed his daughters in a convent where they stayed for six years.

Here, at Oshawa, teaching standards were low and reading was restricted to lives of the saints. But nearby an experimental orchard had been planted for convent use by a French priest. His name was Father Pugh. He was experienced in horticulture and taught little Alice to know many species, and how to make grafts. She also helped to weed the convent garden, to feed the chickens and gather eggs.

The serious child studied by herself, as much as she could with limited facilities; and she learned from the Sisters how to knit, sew, crochet and cook. Once a year there was a truly happy interlude, when the Sisters went on Retreat to the Mother House in Toronto. The Eastwood girls then visited their uncle and his family at Highland Creek. What bliss to see their cousins and all the farm animals—to rove freely in woods and meadows, after the restrictions of convent life!

Like Father Pugh, Dr. Eastwood was an experimental horticulturist. Continually he was growing new vegetables, grafting fruits, and starting flowering plants from seed. He loved the little niece, whom he considered a "born botanist." She shared his failures as well as his successes and, in appreciation, he started her botanical library with a treatise on plants. Her sister Kate received a fairy tale at the same time.

Another pervasive influence over Alice was the French-Canadian nun who taught music at the convent, who instilled a growing love and knowledge of music in her star pupil. This long outlasted the Sister's departure. More than eighty years later, Miss Eastwood told a friend of her sorrow at parting from the gentle soul. Yet even this early grief had been transformed to something of a blessing in her mind. "Since then," said the old lady, "I have never seemed to miss people when they are gone."

When Alice was fourteen the scene of her life shifted completely. Her father sent for her to join him and resume family life in Denver, Colorado. He had acquired a new store. While living quarters were being constructed, the oldest daughter worked as nursegirl for a Frenchman named Jacob Scherrer, to help pay for the new home. She was responsible for a two-year-old and a tiny baby, but had the run of a comprehensive multilingual library when they were asleep. Her starved mind absorbed language as desert sand the rain. She read voraciously and indiscriminately—all through Miss Muhlbach's historical romances, Dumas, dime novels, heavy classics, and scientific treatises.

During that summer she made her first discovery of treasure in the Colorado mountains. On a camping trip with the Scherrer family, she came upon mountain meadows covered in rich profusion with summer-blooming flowers. The experience partook of revelation.

Descended from the mountains, Alice kept house for her family in comfortable quarters behind the store, and attended public school. A perspicacious teacher and fine musician named Anna Palmer introduced her to the delights of choral singing, directed her reading and, in one year, helped her to catch up with her own age and enter high school. With avidity the young girl stored up treasures of the mind and never seemed aware of the fact that her clothes were shabby and her hands reddened by unending chores at home and in the store. As she said in later years, "I always felt superior to such things."

The East Denver High School principal, James H. Baker (later President of the University of Colorado) taught his entire student body in one room. In such a small group Alice Eastwood could not long remain unknown and unappreciated. She was popular with fellow students, received a prize in algebra, and special attention from the principal. All through high school he directed her reading, to include Dickens, Thackeray, Scott. John Burroughs led naturally to Thoreau. Maudsley's "Body and Mind" piqued her interest in the insoluble mysteries of life.

Junior year was eventful. Somewhat to her dismay, she learned that her father planned to marry again, and that she must play second fiddle. But the stepmother was a teacher, a Unitarian from Newburyport, Massachusetts, and a kindly woman. Actually life became easier for Alice, until her father lost money in the new store. Then she went to work again. By studying alone at night, and sometimes consulting her stepmother, she kept up with her class and re-entered it as a senior, to be one of the early graduates of East Denver High School.

To earn her way senior year, she got up at four every morning to lay and light furnace fires in the school building. Afternoons from two to six and all day Saturday she worked in the ready-made dress department of a downtown store for $12 a week. She had apprenticed herself the previous summer, without pay, to be cutter's assistant; so now, by basting linings in basques and working innumerable buttonholes, she managed to pay all her own expenses. And when graduation came, she had friends in two worlds. Elected class valedictorian, she wore a beautiful white silk dress made as a present for her by the girls who worked buttonholes in the ready-made department!

By now Alice Eastwood knew that botany was her calling. Each visit to the mountains confirmed this conviction. Her botanical library was increased by a graduation present of two books, "Flora of Colorado" and Gray's Botany. And a summer job in 1879 led to her first collection of botanical specimens. Through Jacob Scherrer she became shepherd to a flock of pre-schoolers whom she turned into little naturalists. They brought her rocks, insects, birds' eggs, as well as wild flowers, and were good because they were interested. During that summer she also learned to ride horseback, in preparation for field trips.

The immediate necessity of earning a living caused her to apply for a teacher's job, and to start teaching eighth grade and high school Latin. She taught a variety of classes the next few years, including drawing. Often she corrected as many as two hundred compositions a week, in natural science, or history, or English, or American literature, as the case might be. The year she taught astronomy was distinguished by the transit of Venus. This she and her students observed through blackened glasses. She got them out at four in the morning to admire a magnificent comet, and took them on innumerable night expeditions.

On a salary of $475 a year, Alice Eastwood had to skimp to finance the summers she lived for—summers in the Rocky Mountains. Her personal wants were few, and her sole extravagance the buying of botanical books. She made her own clothes. At first she rode side-saddle with a long, voluminous skirt, carrying a long, voluminous nightgown (disguised as a bustle) for over-

night stops. But in time she pioneered among women by design-
ing and making a more sensible denim costume—and riding
astride when she attacked such a mountain as Grays Peak in the
great Continental Divide. This she did several times, and her
summer adventures should inspire an epic saga. Once when her
horse became terrified during an electric storm, most of her
money was scattered and lost. Telling about it afterwards she
confessed, "As a matter of fact, I always had more concern for
my plants than my money!"

These precious plants became the nucleus of the State University's Herbarium at Boulder. Alice Eastwood's own work on the
flora of Colorado was begun when she made her first real botanical discoveries in almost unknown territory. She preferred to
travel alone, but others often wanted to go along, to be guided
by such an erudite and entertaining person. She became increas-
ingly independent in spirit and unconventional in action, scarcely
realizing it until disturbed by an episode unexpectedly tinged
with sadness.

In 1881 she took advantage of low train fares, caused by a railroad rate war, to travel east and visit her Uncle William and his
family at Highland Creek. The old man she found congenial as
ever, but the girl cousins with whom she once had played so happily and freely—these childhood companions had turned into
"high-toned" young ladies who gazed askance at her queer clothes
and shuddered at her strange adventures. Alice Eastwood, eastern Canadian in origin, now longed for her *home* in western
America.

But first, before returning to the now, she traveled farther back in time. At Oshawa she found the orchard cut down, Father Pugh nowhere about, and no Sisters she knew in the convent. She then visited Newburyport, met and enjoyed friends of her stepmother and, eventually, found her way into the inner circle of Cambridge scholars. The Gray Herbarium was on her itinerary, and Asa Gray she met in his own garden. The Botany written by this renowned Harvard professor had been her constant companion during all her summers in the Colorado mountains. With the simplicity and generosity of true greatness, Dr. Gray encouraged his admirer to tell him of her own tiny discoveries, and fired her with true botanical zeal. Alice Eastwood could see, from the eminence of this Cambridge garden, that her mountain time had been play time until now.

Back home again, her most rewarding expedition occurred when she guided the English naturalist, Alfred Russel Wallace, up Grays Peak during alpine flowering season. She possessed his monumental "Malay Archipelago," and was awed by his extensive and penetrative knowledge of distant oceanic islands. Darwin's contemporary who had designated the "Wallace Line" separating the flora and fauna of Asia and Australia—this world figure interrupted his American lecture tour to go skylarking in the Rockies with a young woman in her twenties, as yet unknown to the world! The catalyzer in this unlikely episode was the high school principal, James Baker, who recognized the two as congenial spirits—though separated by forty years in age, a continent and an ocean in locale.

During a complete decade Alice Eastwood divided her life between avocation (at which she earned her living) and vocation

—spending Denver winters with her students and summers among the Colorado flora. Her salary rose to $100 a month, and her botanical library and herbarium increased in size. She also managed to save enough to buy a lot in downtown Denver, going in with her father. When there was a real estate boom she sold her share for $10,000.

"I felt like a millionaire," Miss Eastwood confessed to Mrs. Wilson. With a keen business sense, she then invested $5,000 in a building with her father; bought two more lots and built two small houses for rent income, all this for the remaining $5,000! "Now," triumphantly she told herself, "I can retire and devote all the rest of my life to Botany!"

From reading, she decided that Ponce de Leon was right, Florida must truly be the "Land of Flowers." She accompanied an ailing friend on a train headed that way. But it was a year of a big freeze, and she found seashells far more plentiful than flowers. Leaving the beautiful beaches after a few weeks, she visited St. Augustine and started north on her first sea voyage—from Jacksonville to Charleston, South Carolina. Here she switched back to train travel, destination Washington, D. C. She called on fellow botanists in the National Herbarium; and also took in the art galleries, seeing great paintings and sculpture for the first time. She attended concerts, and several sessions of the Senate.

Cincinnati was her next stop—where Alice Eastwood added to her enjoyment of untamed beauty a lasting appreciation of the art of landscaping and plant cultivation. She reveled in planned gardens abounding with spring bulbs in full bloom, lilies-of-the-valley, crocus, tulips, daffodils and hyacinths. This new interest would have its most tangible manifestation when she helped to plan and plant Golden Gate Park, and the floral "Magic Carpet" on Treasure Island, in San Francisco Bay.

California she eventually reached by accompanying and caring for an old lady with a broken hip whose destination was San Diego. This seaside town beloved by invalids became Alice Eastwood's temporary home. She was quite free to wander over *mesas* and explore the *arroyos;* and she carried two prized books with her, "Botany of the California Geological Survey," which she had purchased from the Gray Herbarium, and Asa Gray's own "Synoptical Flora." She had read tantalizing scraps of the lives of early adventurer-botanists who collected along this coast. She resolved someday to fill in gaps of biographical information and write her own account of such intrepid scientists as Archibald Menzies, Thomas Coulter, Thomas Nuttall and the Scot, David Douglas, after whom so very many kinds of plants have been named. This study would take form and eventually be published as "Early Botanical Explorers on the Pacific Coast, and the Trees They Found There."

Alice Eastwood contributed to botanical magazines and met contemporary botanists of note like C. R. Orcutt and Daniel Cleveland, a pioneer San Diego botanist who had assisted Brewer on the Geological Survey. With Kate Sessions, the well-known nursery-woman, she formed a lifelong friendship. But her new friends were not all botanically bent. In San Diego, as everywhere else that she went, Alice Eastwood entered more than one world.

A specific study of trees (not to materialize until 1905 in "A Handbook of the Trees of California") drew the young botanist north to Santa Cruz, where Menzies first sighted the Coast Redwood. Breaking the trip was a stopover in Pasadena. Friends of friends took Miss Eastwood on a picnic to Altadena's poppy fields; and also to call on Mrs. Ezra Carr at her home in "Carmelita Gardens," near the intersection of Orange Grove Avenue and Colorado Street. Here, among plants and trees from all over the world, she saw her first *Sequoia gigantea*. This had been brought down from the Sierra and planted by John Muir, whose lifelong friend and mentor was Jeanne Carr. Wife of a one-time Berkeley professor, Mrs. Carr had friends in the Bay region to whom she referred her young visitor from Colorado.

Santa Cruz lived up to expectations, as did redwood and madrone. But Alice Eastwood's final goal was San Francisco. She arrived in mid-May, 1891, to find the California Academy of Sciences in the midst of moving to its own new headquarters on Market Street between Fifth and Sixth. The past fifteen years had been spent in inadequate, rented space. A new era of expansion seemed at hand, in which Botany as well as other Academy departments would be benefited.

With characteristic directness and disregard of unimportant details, she pressed through the mess of moving and ascended to the sixth floor botanical work rooms. Quickly she found the people she wanted to find—Katharine Brandegee, Curator of Botany, and her husband with whom she edited and published the biological magazine *Zoe*, meaning "Life." Miss Eastwood wanted to become a botanical writer and this already (in its second year) was the best outlet in the West. Also the Academy had pioneered in recognition and encouragement of women scientists. As early as 1853 Dr. Albert Kellogg, one of the founders, had introduced a resolution to that effect.

Although they had not met before, the young botanist frequently had encountered the name of Brandegee in her well-worn Gray's Botany and Coulter's Manual. As botanist with Hayden's Survey in the '70's, T. S. Brandegee collected and named many species found in Colorado. During the interview Miss Eastwood secured an assignment to write an article for *Zoe*, plus an invitation for Sunday lunch. Several Sundays she went on botanical expeditions with the congenial pair, including one unforgettable ascent of Mount Tamalpais in Marin County, where one day she would have a week-end home and growing ground.

The California visit in 1891 was followed by a return to Colorado, and a summer spent in and around cliff dweller ruins. Alice Eastwood's "Notes on the Cliff Dwellers" appeared in *Zoe*, January '93. Her first article for that magazine was called "The Common Shrubs of Southern Colorado." It came out in July '91, along with advice on "The Fertilization of Geraniums." The Brandegees were delighted with their versatile new feature writer and begged her to return for the winter, to help organize the Academy Herbarium. For this purpose she extended her leave from East Denver High School, finding Principal Baker cooperative as always.

Living on a salary of $50 a month in an unheated room, working in inadequately heated and furnished quarters at the Academy, she could warm herself with summer memories of mountain meadows. The October issue of *Zoe* contained a paean of praise for the "Mariposa Lilies of Colorado" commencing:

"So distinct, so individual are those blossoms that they seem to have souls. They speak a wonderfully enticing language to draw the wandering insects to their honeyed depths . . . the bands of color on both divisions of the perianth are bewildering, impossible to describe; but more than aught else, they cause each flower to say proudly, with uplifted head, 'I am myself; there is no other like me.'

"To see the different kinds of insects hovering over these plants, alighting on the flowers and crawling slowly through the viscid hairs of the honey glands is to understand how this race of lovely hybrids came to be. Not in vain do these flowers set off their beauty and store their sweets."

A "biological" magazine, as *Zoe* professed to be, seemed custom-made for Alice Eastwood. She enjoyed reading and writing essays on a variety of subjects, such as appeared in *Zoe* during its decade of publication. Contents in the bound volumes include dissertations by authorities on "The Strange Nesting Place of the Barn Owl," "The Vegetation of 'Burns,'" "Ferns of Tamalpais," "Studies Among Mollusks," "Notes on the Land Mammals of California," "The Cape Region of Baja California."

The Brandegees tried hard to keep Miss Eastwood in San Francisco beyond her allotted time. In April '92 she was elected a resident member of the California Academy of Sciences, and assigned responsibility (to help support *Zoe*) in founding the

California Botanical Club, whose activities she directed ever after. But she had no thought of permanent severance from the Colorado scene.

She wanted to write, at home, and continue to spend her summers in the mountains, going on exciting expeditions and collecting rare botanical specimens for her own herbarium. An exploratory trip through a little-known section of the Great American Desert was next on schedule. The winter she would divide between her family, her students, and her writing. A full-length book was nearing completion, after years of preparation. This she finally published at her own expense, calling it "Popular Flora of Denver, Colorado." She lost a good deal of money on the venture, knowing nothing of promotional methods, and so enraged her father that he burned a large pile of unsold copies which were cluttering up their small home.

Perhaps for consolation, his oldest daughter then joined a Philosophy seminar presided over by a Unitarian minister and meeting in the living-room of the Denver Librarian, John Cotton Dana. Presently, as a commission, she arranged a botanical portfolio of local plants for the Public Library. From time to time she sent presents to her friends in San Francisco, including five rare birds' eggs and two nests, as well as carefully mounted herbarium specimens.

At summer's end in '92, Katharine Brandegee wrote offering Alice Eastwood her own salary of $75 a month if she would return to the California Academy of Sciences as Joint-Curator of Botany. She added that her husband's resources now made it possible for them both to work there without pay. The prospect of daily association with such congenial spirits, such unworldly and whole-souled scientists; the proximity of a fine reference library and comprehensive herbarium—these were attractions hard to resist.

After nursing her sister Kate through typhoid, Alice Eastwood came at last to live in San Francisco, in December 1892. She was thirty-three years old, in the full bloom of young womanhood, already recognized nationally as a field botanist and essayist on botanical subjects. The appointment was a popular one, and she received a heart-warming welcome on the West Coast.

A year later the Brandegees left the Academy forever and moved to San Diego, taking their own botanical library and private herbarium which had served the institution so well during a difficult transition period. Alice Eastwood succeeded the wife as Curator of Botany, and the husband as acting editor of *Zoe*. This dual responsibility she took very seriously. According to her biographer, "She was the only person who understood haphazard Brandegee methods. Her orderly mind offended by lack of system, she set herself sternly at the task of organizing the accumulation of years of collecting. Far into the night, week after week, she patiently prepared proper labels . . . . Thousands of invaluable specimens of early California plants were then mounted in accessible form," for the use of hundreds of students through the years.

Periodic collecting trips relieved the tedium of curatorial tasks. Katharine Brandegee had arranged an unlimited railroad pass for her friend and, beyond railway terminals, Alice Eastwood traveled by stage, on horseback and afoot. In due time, the automobile and airplane eased her transportation problem. She went on notable expeditions up Mount Shasta, to Del Norte County, the Santa Lucia Mountains, and interior valleys in California; besides to Oregon, Alaska, Nevada, Utah, New Mexico, Baja California—returning always with valuable additions to the Academy collection.

The Bay region she explored thoroughly, from "The Flora of the Nob Hill Cobblestones" to the wooded slopes of Mount Tamalpais. Southern California native plants and trees became best known to her through a long-time affiliation with the Rancho Santa Ana Botanic Garden founded by Susanna Bixby Bryant in memory of John Bixby, her pioneer father. In the Santa Ana Canyon, where Miss Eastwood went faithfully in spring and fall for councilors' meetings, she encountered a former student of Dr. Jepson from Berkeley, employed as the Garden Botanist. This was Tom Howell, who later became her companion on many botanizing expeditions, her associate in the publication of *Leaflets of Western Botany* and, finally, her successor as Curator of Botany at the Academy. Miss Eastwood's long and understanding friendship with this much younger person rivals the most satisfactory mother-son relationship.

The only break in Miss Eastwood's ceaseless activity at the California Academy of Sciences, during her fifty-seven-year tenure of office there, occurred in April 1906—as a result of San Francisco's catastrophic earthquake and fire—and lasted until the Academy constructed and moved into permanent headquarters in Golden Gate Park. The institution rose like the city, from ruins and ashes. Meanwhile Alice Eastwood spent six years in study at the great herbaria of the Smithsonian Institution in Washington, D. C., the New York Botanical Garden and Arnold Arboretum near Boston; also in London's Kew Gardens and British Museum, the University of Cambridge, and Jardin des Plantes in Paris.

Returning home in June 1912 to participate in the Academy's reopening in magnificent new buildings, Alice Eastwood found herself a legend—a celebrated heroine of the great disaster. Her own account of course is modest, but she is credited with saving complete Academy records and irreplaceable botanical type specimens which became the nucleus of all the collections that nowadays distinguish the Academy's botanical department. This feat was accomplished by extreme personal risk, while the Market Street building was collapsing from earthquakes and threatened by fire. Her personal possessions she unhesitatingly consigned to the flames, save for a favorite pocket lens.

Contributing to "Science" only a few weeks later (in May 1906), describing the destruction of the Academy and most of its collections, she wrote: "I do not feel the loss to be mine, but it is a great loss to the scientific world and an irreparable loss to California. My own destroyed work I do not lament, for it was a joy to me while I did it, and I still can have the same joy in starting it again . . . to me came the chance to care for what was saved from the ruins of the Academy, and with the help of my devoted friends I was able to do it."

This indomitable spirit characterized Alice Eastwood through each era of a long lifetime. Lately lying in bed, mortally ill, she would reassure her visitors, "Of course I'll get well. I've always been a healthy person." Approaching ninety-five, she said, "I count my age by friends, and I am rich in friends."

Finis

Early Botanical Explorers
on the Pacific Coast
and the Trees They Found There

by ALICE EASTWOOD

ALICE EASTWOOD'S BOOKPLATE
Presented on her eightieth birthday
by members of the California Botanical Club.
The familiar vista of her beloved
MT. TAMALPAIS
was drawn by Alice B. Chittenden

Early Botanical Explorers
on the Pacific Coast
and the Trees They Found There

The Earliest Botanical Specimens
from the New World

LONG BEFORE anything was known of the flora of the Northwest Coast of North America, plants useful to man had been introduced from South America into the gardens of Europe by the Spanish explorers and conquerors. Columbus was the first, for when he returned to Spain in 1492, after his famous discovery of a new world, he brought back seeds which had been given to him by an Indian who called them "maize." Since the Spanish and Portuguese were the greatest navigators of that time, Indian corn was early distributed to remote parts of the known world, and because of its wide distribution its American origin has been doubted.[1] When he returned to England in 1580 from his voyage around the world, Francis Drake also brought back plants which were named and some of them illustrated by Clusius[2] in *Atrobatis Exoticorum* in 1605. The flora of the Eastern United States had also become known, many species having been described by Linnaeus.[3]

23

The La Pérouse Expedition

In 1785 an expedition was sent out by the French Government, under the command of Jean-François Galaup de La Pérouse, who was noted for his prowess in war, his noble character and his efficiency in all he undertook. It was well equipped to continue and increase what had been learned from the voyage of Captain James Cook; and able scientists in geology, botany, geography and astronomy eagerly joined the expedition. During their stay at Monterey, in September, 1786, the gardener-botanist, Collignon, sent seeds of a lovely herbaceous plant to the Jardin des Plantes, where they were planted. This, the first plant from California to be grown in the Old World, proved to be the rose-colored Sand Verbena, common on the coast of California. It was named *Abronia* by Jussieu[4] and later Lamarck[5] named it *Abronia umbellata*. Collignon also sent a cone containing ripe seeds, and from them twelve trees were grown in the Jardin des Plantes. The pine was named *Pinus californica*. Since the exact locality was uncertain and the trees were no longer living, what was probably the Monterey Pine was later named from the collection of Thomas Coulter, *Pinus radiata*. La Pérouse's last letter was from Botany Bay. The exact fate of the expedition is unknown, but many years later relics were found on one of the small islands of the New Hebrides and were taken to Paris, where I unexpectedly ran across them in the Louvre in 1911.[6]

An expedition sent out by the Spanish Government, under the command of Alejandro Malaspina, left Spain in July, 1789, on a voyage of discovery.[7] One of the objects was to find a passage from the Pacific to the Atlantic. The botanists accompanying the expedition were Luis Neé and Thaddeus Haenke, both well trained in their science. Haenke, who seems to have been the only botanist at Monterey, which the expedition reached in 1791, collected the California Fuchsia (*Zauschneria californica*) and *Datisca glomerata*. The Coast Live Oak (*Quercus agrifolia*) and the Valley Oak (*Quercus lobata*) were named by Neé from specimens brought to him from Monterey by two of the ship's officers, but most of the botanical collecting was done in Mexico and South America. After Haenke's death several years later in Peru, *Reliquiae Haenkeanae* was published by Presl from his notes and drawings.[8] It is one of the most valuable publications on the flora of South America.

VANCOUVER AND MENZIES

Vancouver's voyage around the world in the years 1790 to 1795 was most important in bringing plants from the Pacific Coast of North America to the notice of the world. Archibald Menzies, botanist and surgeon of the expedition, was not only a well-trained botanist, a graduate of the University of Edinburgh, but also a cultured gentleman. His journal is in the possession of the British Museum. The part pertaining to Oregon, Washington and British Columbia was published in 1923, in the *Archives of British Columbia*, Memoir No. 5, and that covering California was published in the *Quarterly* of the California Historical Society, Vol. II, No. 4, January, 1924. In the former is given a list of the species credited to him in the North. As he was in California in the late fall and early winter months only, he made but few collections, and the specimens were generally either too old or too young for satisfactory naming. All that could be identified from his descriptions in his journal were named by myself.

Menzies was the first to collect the Coast Redwood[9] which he found at Santa Cruz.[A]* Specimens were sent to Lambert and named by him *Taxodium sempervirens*.[10] One of them is in the Herbarium of the British Museum, where I had the privilege of seeing it. Menzies discovered the Douglas Spruce on the shores of Nootka Sound in 1792, and also the Nootka Cypress (*Chamaecyparis nootkatensis*); the Madroño (*Arbutus Menziesii*) near Vancouver; and the California Laurel (*Umbellularia californica*) in California. At Sitka he was the first to collect the Sitka Spruce (*Picea sitchensis*), the Oregon Cedar (*Thuja plicata*) and the Hemlock Spruce (*Tsuga Mertensiana*). These were not named from Menzies' specimens, but from those of Mertens[11] by Bongard.[12] Menzies' specimens were not always named at once, and many first collected by him were named from collections made later by others. Indeed, some of Menzies' specimens today are in the Herbarium of the British Museum still unnamed. I feel sure that from seeds of the Yellow Bush Lupine collected by him, the plants were raised to which the name *Lupinus arboreus* was given by Sims in the *Botanical Magazine*, plate 682, with locality unknown.[13] About the same time it was growing in the Botanic Garden at Oxford. The fruiting specimen collected by Menzies was later named *Lupinus macrocarpus*, showing that it was in fruit. There has been some mystery about the tobacco which he

*Notes "A" to "F" have been added by John Thomas Howell.

collected and reported as smoked by the Indians. At the Royal Herbarium at Kew is a specimen consisting of some root leaves which differ in shape from any of the native species of North America. In the Herbarium of the British Museum is a specimen collected by Captain George Dixon, from Queen Charlotte Island, as Indian Tobacco. It is badly mutilated by insects and consists of the upper flowering part of a stem. The only perfect leaf resembles those of Menzies' specimen, and the only good flower differs from the flowers of all other native tobaccos. As Menzies was on Queen Charlotte Island when Captain Dixon was there (on a previous voyage with Captain Colnett), I feel convinced that the two specimens represent a still-unnamed *Nicotiana*.[14]

Vancouver was not always fair to Menzies. The man who was supposed to care for the living plants which Menzies had in a glass case Vancouver assigned to other duties; and on the second visit to San Francisco when the expedition was not so hospitably received, he would not allow Menzies to leave the boat. After their return to England he demanded that Menzies deliver his journal to him, but Menzies refused and referred him to the officials of the British Museum who were the real owners.

Karl Heinrich Mertens was born in Germany and was well educated, especially in botany, for his father (Franz Karl Mertens) was a well-known botanist in whose honor the genus *Mertensia* is named. He was keen to explore and tried to join the Kotzebue expedition but failed. Later he joined another under Captain Feodor P. Lütke. Among the places visited was the island of Sitka. From Mertens' Sitka collections Bongard wrote his

Flora Sitchensis,[15] in which some of our Californian coast trees were named. He collected both species of *Tsuga* (or *Pinus*, as they were then called), one named *P. Mertensiana* and the other *P. canadensis*. The latter was supposed to be the same as the eastern species. He also collected the Coast Spruce, *Picea sitchensis*, and the Coast Alder, *Alnus rubra*. There was confusion concerning the identity of *Tsuga Mertensiana* until Professor C. S. Sargent, of the Arnold Arboretum, identified it with what had been known in California as *Tsuga Pattoniana*, the lovely Hemlock Spruce of the Sierra Nevada. What was considered *T. canadensis* is now known as *T. heterophylla*. Menzies was the first to discover and collect specimens of these trees, but they were named from the collections of Mertens.

THE KOTZEBUE EXPEDITION

The next important expedition was that sent out by the Russians in 1815 under Captain Otto von Kotzebue in the *Rurik*, which had been fitted out by Count Nikolai Petrovitch Romanzoff.[16] Two eminent scientists were aboard: Adelbert von Chamisso and Johann Friedrich Eschscholtz. The former was of French parentage but born and reared in Germany. Not only was he known as an able botanist, but also as a poet and the author of the story of Peter Schlemihl who sold his shadow to the devil. Eschscholtz was interested in all branches of natural history, especially entomology. They were in San Francisco, Bodega, San Jose and Monterey in 1816. Most of their collections were made in San Francisco, probably at the Presidio. Their species could be found there forty years ago, but have been killed by the dense forest of cypress, pine and eucalyptus planted years ago, and more recently by the *Mesembryanthemum*. The following list of plants named by them, or named by others from their collections, may be of interest: *Abronia latifolia* (Yellow Sand Verbena), *Ceanothus thyrsiflorus* (California Lilac), *Eschscholtzia californica* (California Poppy), *Hypericum anagalloides* (Swamp St. John's-wort), *Lupinus Chamissonis* (Blue Bush Lupine), *Frankenia grandifolia* (Salt-weed), *Rhamnus californica* (Coffee-berry), *Horkelia californica*, *Aster Chamissonis*, *Lessingia germanorum*, *Franseria Chamissonis*, *Eriophyllum artemisiaefolium* (Golden Yarrow), *Tanacetum camphoratum* (Tansy), *Artemisia californica*, *Phacelia malvaefolia*, *Micromeria Chamissonis* (Yerba Buena), *Myrica californica* (Wax Myrtle), *Cryptantha Chorisiana* (White Forget-me-not), *Rubus ursinus* and *Rubus vitifolius* (Blackberry), *Solanum umbelliferum* (Blue Nightshade), *Scrophularia californica* (Bee-plant).[B]

ANOTHER RUSSIAN COLLECTION

Extensive collections were made by others; and seeds of many of the trees which had been named from the specimens collected by Menzies, Douglas and others, were sent to the Imperial Botanic Garden at St. Petersburg (as it was then known) and distributed to other countries. A collection made by I. G. Vosnesensky in 1840 and 1841 was recently discovered and sent to the Arnold Arboretum for determination. Mr. John Thomas Howell, of the California Academy of Sciences, was asked to name the specimens and undertook the interesting task. If these had been named when received, many species of Californian plants would today have

different names, probably more difficult to spell and to pro-
nounce.[17] This set of plants had been lost for one hundred years,
and before being named had gone around the world. Vosnesensky
was in the party that ascended Mount St. Helena when that
mountain received its name.[18] Collections were made at Bodega
Bay and at Fort Ross. In 1904 I went by sea to Bodega Bay to
follow the route of the many expeditions that had sought the
shelter of that harbor. An iron ring was still to be seen where the
old wharf had been, and outside the fence surrounding the point
the flowers grew as when the Russians saw them.

DAVID DOUGLAS

The most important collections on the Pacific Coast were made
by the dauntless David Douglas.[19] He began his career as a gardener's apprentice, but became so greatly interested in plants that
when he went to Glasgow to work in the Botanic Garden, he at-
tracted the attention of Sir William J. Hooker, Professor of
Botany at Glasgow University. He accompanied him on botanical excursions; and when the London Horticultural Society was
looking for someone to send on an expedition in search of new
plants for the gardens of Great Britain, Sir William Hooker
recommended David Douglas. He visited the Columbia River
region in 1825 and 1829, and in December, 1830, he made a
journey to Monterey and remained in California until August,
1832. To enumerate all the species that he collected as botanical
specimens, the seeds of plants which were raised in the garden of
the Society and distributed to members, and named chiefly by
John Lindley, would fill a book. After his tragic death in the

Hawaiian Islands, a sketch of his journeys in North America and some of his letters were published in Hooker's *Companion to the Botanical Magazine*.[20] In 1914 some of this material was republished, together with his complete journal, by the Royal Horticultural Society of England.[21] That he was able to collect what he did seems incredible when one reads of the hardships that he endured—rain day after day, often without food, and in continual danger from the Indians. He never gave up, even when he became ill, but tried above all to keep his specimens and seeds from spoiling. An enumeration of the trees alone can be given. Many were named from botanical specimens collected by him and from which seeds were planted. *Taxus brevifolia* (Yew), *Juniperus occidentalis* (Mountain Juniper), *Pinus Lambertiana* (Sugar Pine), *P. contorta* (Coast Pine), *P. monticola* (Mountain Pine), *P. ponderosa* (Yellow Pine), *P. Sabiniana* (Digger Pine), *P. radiata* (Monterey Pine), *Abies amabilis* (Lovely Fir), *A. grandis* (Coast Fir), *A. nobilis* (Noble Fir), and the Santa Lucia Fir (*A. venusta*).[c] Among the oaks, he discovered *Quercus Garryana* (Garry Oak), *Q. Douglasii* (Douglas Oak), *Q. densiflora* (Tanbark Oak, now known as *Lithocarpus*). He discovered *Castanopsis chrysophylla* (Chinquapin) and *Negundo californica* (Box Elder), also known as Maple. It took him fifteen hours to climb the mountain, near the cascades of the Columbia River, where he found the two mountain firs, because the brush was so dense and the trees were in an unbroken forest.[22]

The following extracts from his journal tell of some of his trials and show his character:

1826. Sunday, January 1st.—Commencing a year in such a far re-moved corner of the earth, where I am nearly destitute of civilised society, there is some scope for reflection. In 1824, I was on the Atlantic on my way to England; 1825, between the island of Juan Fernandez and the Galapagos in the Pacific; I am now here [at Fort Vancouver], and God only knows where I may be the next. In all probability, if a change does not take place, I will shortly be consigned to the tomb. I can die satisfied with myself. I never have given cause for remonstrance or pain to an in-dividual on earth. I am in my twenty-seventh year.[23]

In November, while in what is now western Oregon, he wrote:

Saturday, 11th.—Last night, after lying down to sleep, we began to dispute about the road, I affirming we were two or three miles off our way, they that we were quite close to our former encampment; all tenacious of our opinions. The fact plainly this: all hungry and no means of cooking a little of our stock; travelled thirty-three miles, drenched and bleached with rain and sleet, chilled with a piercing north wind; and then to finish the day experienced the cooling, comfortless consolation of lying down wet without supper or fire. On such occasions I am very liable to become fretful.[24]

The following is an account of his collecting the Sugar Pine which he named *Pinus Lambertiana* in honor of the author of Lambert's *Pinetum* in which many Pacific coast coniferae were first described.

Thursday [October] 26th [1826] I left my camp [near the Umpqua River in Oregon] this morning at daylight on an excursion, leaving my guide to take care of the camp and horses until my return in the evening, when I found everything as I wished; in the interval he had dried my wet paper as I desired him. About an hour's walk from my camp I was met by an Indian, who on discovering me strung his bow and placed on his left arm a sleeve of racoon-skin and stood ready on the defence. As I was well convinced this was prompted through fear, he never before having seen such a being, I laid my gun at my feet on the ground and waved my hand for him to come to me, which he did with great caution. I made him place his bow and quiver beside my gun, and then struck a light and gave him to smoke and a few beads. With my pencil I made a rough sketch of the cone and pine I wanted and showed him it, when he instantly pointed to the hills about fifteen or twenty miles to the south. As I wanted to go in that direction, he seemingly with much good-will went with me. At midday I reached my long-wished Pinus (called by the Umpqua tribe *Natele*), and lost no time in examining and endeavouring to collect specimens and seeds. New or strange things seldom fail to make great impressions, and often at first we are liable to over-rate them; and lest I should never see my friends to tell them verbally of this most beautiful and immensely large tree, I now state the dimensions of the largest one I could find that was blown down by the wind: Three feet from the ground, 59 feet 9 inches in circumference; 134 feet from the ground, 17 feet 5 inches; extreme length, 215 feet. The trees are remarkably straight; bark uncommonly smooth for such large timber, of a whitish or light brown colour; and yields a great quantity of gum of a bright amber colour. The large trees are destitute of branches, generally for two-thirds the length of the tree; branches pendulous, and the cones hanging from their points like small sugar-loaves in a grocer's shop, it being only on the very largest trees that cones are seen, and the putting myself in possession of three cones (all I could) nearly brought my life to an end. Being unable to climb or hew down any, I took my gun and was busy clipping them from the branches with ball when eight Indians came at the report of my gun. They were all painted with red earth, armed with bows, arrows, spears of bone, and flint knives, and seemed to me anything but friendly. I endeavoured to explain to them what I wanted and they seemed satisfied and sat down to smoke, but had no sooner done so than I perceived one string his bow and another sharpen his flint knife with a pair of wooden pincers and hang it on the wrist of the right hand, which gave me ample testimony of their inclination. To save myself I could not do by flight, and without any hesitation I went backwards six paces and cocked my gun, and then pulled from my belt one of my pistols, which I held in my left hand. I was determined to fight for life. As I as much as possible endeavoured to preserve my coolness and perhaps did so, I stood eight or ten minutes looking at them and they at me without a word passing, till one at last, who seemed to be the leader, made a sign for tobacco, which I said they should get on condition of going and fetching me some cones. They went, and as soon as out of sight I picked up my three cones and a few twigs, and made a quick retreat to my camp, which I gained at dusk. The Indian who undertook to be my guide I sent off, lest he should betray me. Wood of the pine, fine, and very heavy; leaves short, in five, with a very short sheath bright green; cones, one 14½ inches long, one 14, and one 13½, and all containing fine seed.[25]

Douglas' California journal was lost in a shipwreck on the Fraser River in 1833,[26] so we know very little about his collecting in California,[27] but it must have been very easy compared to his trials in the north. He collected around Monterey, San Francisco and Santa Barbara. I feel sure that he must have been on Mount Diablo, because he collected *Calochortus pulchellus* which has never been found elsewhere. For a long time it was confused with the other yellow globe tulip which was named by Carl Purdy, *Calochortus amabilis*, when I showed him the Mount Diablo flowers.

OTHER BOTANICAL EXPLORERS

Thomas Coulter was born at Dundalk, in Ireland, and became interested in natural history when quite young. He was educated at Trinity College, Dublin, and was especially noted for his knowledge of botany and entomology. He also studied botany under the elder DeCandolle at Geneva. When he was about thirty, he accepted a position as medical officer to the Real del Monte Mining Company of Mexico for three years. In 1831, he came to Monterey, where he met David Douglas. They collected together until Douglas went to the Hawaiian Islands and Coulter began an overland trip through the Salinas Valley to Southern

California and Arizona. He is said to have collected fifty thousand specimens representing fifteen hundred to two thousand species. His notes and journals were all lost, but his specimens are in the herbarium of Trinity College. He was made curator and spent the rest of his life arranging his collections. He was not interested in introducing plants into cultivation, but only in collecting botanical specimens. However, several important trees were named from his collections. He went into the Santa Lucia Mountains, where he collected the Santa Lucia Fir, the Big-cone Pine (*Pinus Coulteri*) and the Prickle-cone Pine (*Pinus muricata*).[c] Seeds of these were sent by other collectors to England and trees were raised from them, but they were named from Coulter's specimens.[28]

Thomas Nuttall was born in Yorkshire, England, and at an early age was apprenticed to his uncle, a printer. In 1808, when he was 22 years of age, he came to the United States and became associated with the Philadelphia Academy of Sciences. In 1809 and 1811, he and John Bradbury went on an exploring and collecting trip to the Upper Missouri. In 1819, he explored Arkansas territory. In 1834, he joined the Wyeth Oregon expedition, and finally reached Fort Walla Walla on the Columbia River.[29] Difficulties, hardships and dangers did not prevent him from collecting. To transport and dry botanical specimens and the paper in which to collect them under these conditions was extremely hard. It is said that he would sit for hours before a hot camp fire, with the sweat pouring down his face, to dry his papers. In 1836, he came by sea to California and collected at Monterey, Santa Barbara and San Diego. Richard Henry Dana, in *Two Years Before the Mast,* states that he was a passenger on the *Pilgrim* on its return voyage, and that he had formerly occupied the chair of Botany and Ornithology in Harvard University. It is said that, in order to avoid interruptions, he worked in a garret which he entered by a ladder through a trap-door, and after he was securely in, the ladder was pulled up. He made large collections in California, but the chief trees are *Platanus racemosa* (Sycamore), at Santa Barbara; *Aesculus californica* (Buckeye), and *Alnus rhombifolia* (Alder) at Monterey.[D] In Oregon, he was the first to collect the Oregon Ash (*Fraxinus oregona*), also the Blue Elderberry (*Sambucus glauca*), both common in California. Nuttall gave his herbarium to the British Museum, though some of the specimens are in the herbarium of the Philadelphia Academy of Sciences. Many specimens in the British Museum have manuscript names which were never published.

Acer macrophyllum was collected in 1805 in Oregon, on the Great Rapids of the Columbia, by Meriwether Lewis of the Lewis and Clark expedition.

Theodor Hartweg was a German gardener, following the profession of his ancestors. At one time he was employed at the Jardin des Plantes, in Paris, and later he went to England. He was then twenty-four years of age. The London Horticultural Society sent him on a collecting expedition to Mexico, on which he spent seven years and sent back valuable collections of seeds and botanical specimens. In 1845, he was sent to California and spent some time in the region around Monterey. The Monterey Cypress was named *Cupressus macrocarpa* by him. He also discovered *Cupressus Goveniana* at Monterey. Seeds and specimens of

Cupressus macrocarpa had been given to Lambert and named by him but never published, and where the seeds came from was unknown. Hartweg also collected *Quercus chrysolepis*, at Monterey, which was described from his collection. He tried to obtain seeds of the Santa Lucia Fir, *Abies venusta*, but found them frozen. He visited Sonoma, where he discovered *Quercus Kelloggii*. Later he went into the foothills of the Sierra Nevada, near the present site of Marysville, and was the first to make known plants from the Sierra of California. The results of his collection were published by George Bentham under the title, *Plantae Hartwegianae.*[30] In the *Quarterly* of the California Historical Society for December, 1933, is a reference to Hartweg in "The Memoirs of Theodor Cordua."[31] Cordua accompanied Hartweg on trips and gives a lively, interesting account of one they made together to Bear Valley. On this trip, Hartweg collected the Knob-cone Pine (*Pinus attenuata*) and many species well known, such as the prostrate *Ceanothus* (Mahala Mats), *Chamaebatia foliolosa* (Mountain Misery), the yellow-flowered Honeysuckle (*Lonicera interrupta*), the red *Fritillaria recurva* and the common *Brodiaea capitata.*[E]

William Lobb began his career as a gardener, and while in the employ of William Veitch, who had a large nursery at Exeter, England, became greatly interested in botany. He showed such intelligence and ability that Veitch sent him to South America to collect seeds and plants. He was then 31 years of age and spent several years in Mexico, making valuable collections. Veitch next sent him to the Pacific Coast of North America, especially to collect seeds of the trees discovered by Menzies, Coulter, Douglas and others. He landed in San Francisco in 1849. Later he learned through Dr. Albert Kellogg, of the California Academy of Sciences, of the recent discovery of the big trees at Calaveras by a hunter named Dowd. At once he set out to collect specimens and seeds of this remarkable tree. He sent them to England, where the name *Wellingtonia gigantea* was given the tree by the botanist, John Lindley. Dr. Kellogg had sent specimens to Drs. Torrey and Gray and planned to describe and publish it as a new tree, but learned too late of the earlier publication. Lobb was a great collector and succeeded in getting seeds of almost all the trees that had been previously discovered in Western North America, many of which were first introduced to England from his seeds. Several species of plants are named in his honor. He died in San Francisco in 1863 and was buried in Lone Mountain Cemetery (now Laurel Hill).[32] His grave was located by the California Botanical Club several years ago, and the remains were moved to a new location and the grave put in good condition.

John Jeffrey was sent to the Pacific Coast as botanical collector by the Scottish Oregon expedition, about 1850. The members raised the money by subscription, and each one was to receive a portion of the seeds. Jeffrey was expected also to keep a journal but failed to do so. He did very well at first but became neglectful and was later discharged. He collected over five hundred species of plants and sent seeds of most of the trees that had been brought to the notice of the world by earlier explorers. *Pinus Balfouriana, Pinus Jeffreyi* and *Cupressus Lawsoniana* (now called *Chamaecyparis*) were first discovered by Jeffrey.[F] The last was collected on the southern flanks of Mount Shasta. It grows now near Shasta

Springs, which might perhaps be where it was first found. After his discharge, he remained for awhile in California, but did not even visit the Consulate for his letters. Later he joined a party going to Yuma and was never again heard from. The cost of postage on one box is interesting. Sent from San Francisco in 1842, the postage on the box amounted to £135—about $670. However, much to the relief of the subscribers, it was remitted by the postal authorities.[33]

The Incense Cedar (*Libocedrus decurrens*) observed by Frémont in 1844[34] was described by Dr. Torrey in 1853 from specimens obtained by Frémont on the upper waters of the Sacramento in 1846.[35] It did not become well known until 1852, when Jeffrey sent seeds and specimens to Scotland. The name *Thuja Craigiana* was given to it there, and in the gardens of Great Britain it was known by this name.[36] Frémont reported seeing the Sierra Live Oak in March, 1844, on the south fork of the American River, but collected no specimens.[37] It was later described from specimens collected by Dr. F. A. Wislizenus on the American River in 1851, and in 1868 named *Quercus Wislizeni* in his honor.[38] Frémont collected many plants, but made poor specimens, as he was not a botanist. *Fremontia* is named in his honor, besides many species. The localities are often doubtful, as is to be expected in unknown regions where the physical features are unnamed.

THE CALIFORNIA WALNUT

The California Walnut (*Juglans californica*) was first noted in 1837, by Richard Brinsley Hinds, the surgeon and botanist of H.B.M.S. *Sulphur*, which made a voyage around the world in the years 1836-42 under the command of Sir Edward Belcher.[39]

It was late in the autumn of 1837 when an expedition up the Rio Sacramento penetrated from San Francisco to some distance into the interior. ... Occasional clumps of fine oaks and planes imparted an appearance of park land. They were already shedding their leaves; a small grape was very abundant on the banks, and we sometimes obtained a dessert from the fruit of a juglans.[40]

The next reference is that of Torrey in the Botany of the Mexican Boundary Survey, where he mentions a *Juglans* in flower which was found by Dr. Parry at San Fernando beyond Los Angeles.[41] Sereno Watson named the walnut, *Juglans californica*, and stated that it ranges from San Francisco to Southern California.[42] Willis L. Jepson has separated the northern from the southern form, giving the former the name *Juglans Hindsii*, and restricting the latter to *J. californica*.[43]

Notes will be found on pages 43 to 48.

Valedictory

Valedictory

delivered to the Class of '79

by ALICE EASTWOOD

CLASSMATES: For four years we have been together, sharers in the same studies and in the same thoughts. Our pleasant companionship is now at an end, and we are to bid farewell to our schooldays, those happy days which have done so much to fit us for the real duties of life. Our lives, hitherto mingling together so pleasantly, will now be divided—each one starting forth on his own chosen path. Though our paths in life may widely diverge, yet the bond of truth may unite them. If we pursue truth, we shall not wander hither and thither, according to the opinion of men, but move straight forward, and the same goal will be our aim.

There will be found a compensation for all hardships, a solace for all troubles, and a rest from all labors. Joy and sorrow visit all, they are strangers to the lives of none; but may our lives be so ordered that happiness may prevail, and may our troubles be only passing clouds, obscuring for a moment the sun of prosperity. However widely fate may divide us, let the bond of friendship be unbroken; let the memory of these years that we have spent together be preserved, and let our school and everything regarding it ever be an object of affectionate interest.

Good-bye is always a hard word to say, but doubly so when addressed to what we hold dear. With that one word we take leave of the school whose benefits we have received; of the schoolmates, to whose society we owe so many pleasant hours; of our teachers whose care and kindness will never be forgotten, and of one another.*

*The above was found by Mr. Howell among Miss Eastwood's papers, in a torn and yellowed copy of *THE TRIBUNE: Denver, Colorado, Thursday Morning, June 12, 1879*. In that far-off, innocent era the High School Commencement was headlined as "Denver's Delight." Besides the Valedictory, Alice also read her essay on

"Pygmies are Pygmies still, though perched on Alps,
And Pyramids are Pyramids in Vales."

NOTES

1. The *New International Encyclopedia,* under "Maize."

2. Charles de Lecluse, 1526-1609.

3. Carl Linné (usually called by the Latin name, Carolus Linnaeus), a Swedish naturalist (1707-78), proposed new systems of classification in zoology and botany and was the author of many botanical works.

4. Antoine Laurent de Jussieu (1748-1836) was a professor of botany at the Paris Botanical Gardens. His *Genera Plantarum* (1789) laid down the principles upon which modern botanical classification is based.

5. Jean Baptiste Pierre Antoine de Monnet, Chevalier de Lamarck, French naturalist (1744-1829).

6. The records of the first two years and the collections of natural history were sent overland from Kamchatka. From the manuscripts which were saved, four volumes (and an atlas) were published in Paris in 1797 under the title, *Voyage de La Pérouse autour du monde, publié conformément au decret du 22 Avril 1791, et rédigé par M. L. A. Milet-Mureau.* Numerous editions have been issued in English and other languages. The one used in connection with this paper is that published in London in three volumes in 1807.

In 1937 *Le voyage de Lapérouse sur les côtes de l'Alaska et de la Californie (1786),* with an introduction and notes by Gilbert Chinard, was published in Baltimore by the Johns Hopkins Press. In looking over the part relating to Monterey in this volume, I was especially interested in the identity of the plants noted by M. Collignon (on p. 106). My determinations in regard to them are as follows:

L'absinthe maritime, *Artemisia pycnosephala* DC.

L'armoise, *Artemisia heterophylla* Nutt.

Le grand absinthe, probably *Artemisia californica* Less.

L'aurone male, perhaps *Artemisia ludoviciana* Nutt. (This was the identification of the white-downy artemisia related to *A. heterophylla* of Asa Gray in the *Synoptical Flora of North America.*)

La verge d'or du Canada, *Solidago californica* Nutt. Goldenrod.

L'aster (oeil de christ), probably *Aster chilensis* Nees.

La morelle a fruit noir, *Solanum Douglasii* Dunal. Nightshade.

La perce-pierre (criste-marine), *Salicornia ambigua* Michx. Samphire.

La menthe aquatique, probably *Mentha canadensis* L.

Le thé du Mexique, *Micromeria Chamissonis* (Benth.) Greene. Yerba Buena.

La millefeuille, *Achillea Millefolium* L. Milfoil or Yarrow.

7. *Viaje político-científico alrededor del mundo por las corbetas Descubierta y Atrevida al mando de los capitanes de navío, D. Alejandro Malaspina y Don José de Bustamante y Guerra desde 1789 á 1794,* published with an introduction by Pedro de Nova y Colson, Madrid, 1885, gives the account of this expedition. Excerpts from this work were printed in the California Historical Society *Quarterly,* III (Oct. 1924), 215-37.

8. Karel Boriwog (C. B.) Presl, *Reliquiae Haenkeanae,* Prague [1825-36], 2 vols.

9. Malaspina had mentioned "the red pine, a tree much taller than the rest" in the vicinity of Monterey. See the California Historical Society *Quarterly,* III (Oct. 1924), 221.

10. From Aylmer Bourke Lambert, *A Description of the Genus Pinus* (London, 1832), the description of the *Taxodium sempervirens* is quoted by Willis Linn Jepson in his *The Silva of California* (Berkeley, 1910), p. 138.

11. Karl Heinrich Mertens, naturalist of the Luetke expedition, 1827.

12. Heinrich Gustav Bongard (1786-1839), botanist at St. Petersburg.

13. *Curtis's Botanical Magazine* . . . continued by John Sims, M.D., London, 1803, Vol. XVII.

14. See "The Tobacco Collected by Archibald Menzies on the Northwest Coast of America," by Alice Eastwood, in *Leaflets of Western Botany,* Vol. II, No. 6, April, 1938. Menzies' first voyage was made in 1786, when he sailed on the *Prince of Wales,* commanded by Captain Colnett. The ship arrived at Nootka in July, 1787; and early in August, as they were leaving for Alaska, Captain Dixon met them just outside the harbor and persuaded them to accompany him to the Queen Charlotte Islands.

15. "Observations sur la vegetation de L'ile de Sitcha," St. Petersburg Academy of Sciences *Memoirs,* II (1833), 120-77, plates 1-6.

16. Kotzebue's own account of this expedition is given in his *Entdeckungs-Reise in die Sud-See und der Berings-Strasse zur Erforschung einer nord-ostlichen Durchfahrt . . . 1815, 1816, 1817, und 1818 . . . auf dem*

Schiffe Rurick, Weimar, 1821 (3 vols.). It was translated into English and published in London in 1821. Chamisso's account of the voyage was published in Leipzig in 1836 under the title, *Reise um die Welt mit der Romanzoffischen Entdeckungs-Expedition in den Jahren 1815-18 auf der Brigg Rurik.* . . . . Louis Choris, the artist of the expedition, also has recorded the voyage in his *Voyage pittoresque autour du monde,* Paris, 1822. In 1932, the Stanford University Press issued as Vol. II, No. 2, of its *Publications* in History, Economics, and Political Science, *The Visit of the "Rurick" to San Francisco in 1816,* by August C. Mahr, which contains extracts from the works mentioned above. The plants collected by Chamisso are given on pp. 127-77.

17. See "A Russian Collection of Californian Plants," by John Thomas Howell, in *Leaflets of Western Botany,* II (April 19, 1937), 17-20, for an account of this collection.

18. See "Historic Mount Saint Helena," by Honoria Tuomey, in the California Historical Society *Quarterly,* III (July, 1924), 171-77.

19. Names of plants collected by Douglas that are in the herbarium of the Russian Academy of Sciences, Leningrad, are given in "A Collection of Douglas' Western American Plants," by John Thomas Howell, in *Leaflets of Western Botany,* Vol. II, Nos. 4-10, Nov., 1937, to April, 1939.

20. "A Brief Memoir of the Life of Mr. David Douglas, with Extracts from His Letters," in *Companion to the Botanical Magazine,* by Sir W. J. Hooker, London, 1836, II, 79-182.

21. *Journal Kept by David Douglas During His Travels in North America, 1823-1827 . . . with Appendices Containing a List of the Plants and an Account of His Death in 1834,* London: William Wesley & Son, 1914, hereafter cited as Douglas Journal.

22. *Ibid.,* p. 60; *Companion to the Botanical Magazine,* II, p. 93.

23. Douglas Journal, p. 152.

24. *Ibid.,* pp. 235-36.

25. *Ibid.,* pp. 229-31.

26. See Douglas' letter to Hartnell in *Madroño,* 11 (1933), 98-99, and *Leaflets of Western Botany,* II (1937), 61.

27. A letter from Monterey, dated November 23, 1831, was printed in the *Companion to the Botanical Magazine,* II, 149-51, and reprinted in the California Historical Society *Quarterly,* II (Oct. 1923), 223-27,

from a copy in the Douglas correspondence in the Provincial Library at Victoria, B. C. The latter is dated November 20 and differs slightly from the previously printed version.

28. *Veitch's Manual of the Coniferae*, London: James Veitch & Sons, Ltd., 1900, p. 326.

29. In *Madroño*, II (1934), 143-47, is a biographical note on Nuttall by W. L. Jepson entitled, "The Overland Journey of Thomas Nuttall."

30. George Bentham (1839-1894), *Plantae Hartwegianae*, London, 1839-57. The California plants collected by Hartweg in 1846 and 1847 are given on pp. 294-342.

31. Vol. XII, No. 4, pp. 279-311. Cordua's Memoirs were also reprinted in pamphlet form by the California Historical Society.

32. Veitch, *op. cit.*, pp. 243-44.

33. "John Jeffrey and the Oregon Expedition," in *Notes from the Royal Botanic Garden*, XX (Edinburgh, July, 1939), 1-53.

34. John Charles Frémont, *Memoirs of My Life*, Chicago and N. Y., 1887, p. 335.

35. Jepson, *Silva*, p. 149.

36. Veitch, *op. cit.*, p. 254.

37. Frémont, *op. cit.*, p. 345.

38. Jepson, *op. cit.*, p. 232. Adolph Wislizenus (1810-89) was a physician and botanist of German birth who came to America in 1835 and to California for a brief visit in 1851.

39. *Narrative of a Voyage Round the World, Performed in Her Majesty's Ship Sulphur, During the Years 1836-1842*, by Sir Edward Belcher, London, 1843, II, 347.

40. Jepson, *op. cit.*, p. 196, quoting from the preface to Bentham's *Botany of the Sulphur*.

41. *United States and Mexican Boundary Survey*, 1859, Part I, p. 205.

42. American Academy of Arts and Sciences, *Proceedings*, 1857, X, 349.

43. University of California Agricultural Experiment Station *Bulletin*, No. 203 (1909), p. 27.

ADDITIONAL NOTES *by John Thomas Howell*

A. That material of the Redwood was brought to Spain by Malaspina now appears most certain. Trees at Granada, because of their size and apparent age, must certainly have been grown from seed collected as early as the Malaspina Expedition. See "Sequoia sempervirens in Granada," *Madroño,* I (Sept., 1929), 242.

B. Kotzebue was in command of two Russian expeditions which visited the west coast of North America, the first in the *Rurik* as described by Miss Eastwood which visited California in 1816, the second in the *Predpriatie* which visited San Francisco in 1824. Chamisso and Eschscholtz were the naturalists in 1816, with Chamisso attending to the botanical collections. In 1824, Eschscholtz alone was naturalist and it was from his own collections that he named such well-known California plants as the Yellow Sand Verbena, California Lilac and Coffee-berry. See "The Botanical Collections of Chamisso and Eschscholtz in California," by Alice Eastwood, in *Leaflets of Western Botany,* IV (April 28, 1944), 17-21; *Marin Flora,* p. 29, by John Thomas Howell (1949).

C. Among the trees listed by Miss Eastwood as having been named from specimens collected by David Douglas is the Monterey Pine. This well-known California pine received two names about the same time: *Pinus radiata* D. Don, the older and acceptable name, based on a collection made by Thomas Coulter at Monterey; and *Pinus insignis* Douglas, published later and based on Douglas' own collection.

In this connection it is interesting to note the relation of Coulter and Douglas to the Santa Lucia Fir. Coulter was the first botanist to discover this remarkable endemic and it was perhaps he who told Douglas where it could be found. But when it came to the naming of it, Douglas came out ahead—that is why the tree is called *Abies venusta* (the name based on Douglas' collection) and not *Abies bracteata* (the name based on Coulter's collection).

D. Although Thomas Nuttall is the author of the name *Aesculus californica,* that early botanical visitor to California did not make the original collection as is inferred by Miss Eastwood. The California Buckeye was first collected by Paolo Emilio Botta, naturalist on a French expedition which visited California in 1827. His material was the basis for a new genus and species, *Calothyrsus californicus*, but it was Nuttall who recognized the true generic affinity of the tree and referred it to *Aesculus*. In California botany, Botta is commemorated in the name of our Farewell-to-spring, *Godetia Bottae;* and in ornithology he is remembered as the first collector of the California Road-runner. Botta did not pursue natural history as his life work but became interested in archaeology and his fame in that field rests on his excavation of the ruins of Nineveh. See "Early Naturalists in the Far West," by Roland H. Alden and John D. Ifft, in *Occasional Papers of the California Academy of Sciences*, XX (April 30, 1943), 31, 32.

E. The original collection of the Knob-cone Pine, *Pinus attenuata*, was made by Theodor Hartweg in the Santa Cruz Mountains, not in the Sierra Nevada. According to Sargent, the pine Hartweg collected in Bear Valley was *P. contorta* var. *Murrayana*. See "Notes on West American Coniferae," by J. G. Lemmon, in *Erythea*, I (Nov., 1893), 229-231; Charles Sprague Sargent, *The Silva of North America*, XI (1897), 91.

F. According to Sargent, the Lawson Cypress was first discovered by Mr. William Murray "on the south flanks of Mt. Shasta in California . . . in the autumn of 1854," Sargent, *Silva*, X (1890), 120. However, the original specimens of the Lodgepole Pine, *Pinus Murrayana*, named in honor of Andrew Murray, were collected in the Siskiyou Mountains by Jeffrey. Sargent, *Silva*, XI (1897), 93.

2000 Copies

Designed and printed by Lawton Kennedy

January 1954